Michael Andrew Law
Artist Statement
「藝術家自述」

My paintings tries to captured the Soul of Youth , I combines classical mediums such as Pigment & Oil with contemporary painting method and medium such as Digital CG as Giclée Prints , I Only interested on ONE but immortal subject matters : Female Figures, by set against the figures with chinese calligraphy Employing the Idea of Word as Image, as an expressive scenario . I use both Life models and Computer Generated Images for the creation of works .

Through juxtaposition, both Icons (The Words and Female figures) , Both added meanings to the other.

These paintings are My Own interpret and to document HongKong's own Millennial and its Generation's view point and identities : As "Hongkonger".

oil on canvas 30x30"

oil on canvas 32x46"

oil on canvas 9x4'

Michael Andrew Law at Work.

Michael Andrew Law

Michael Andrew Law (Born Law Cheuk Yui) was born 1982 in British Hong Kong. After studying Classical oil painting private lessons with New York Artist Daniel Anderson (1928 - 2008) at the his then-new workshop in Hong Kong, he made a stunning reputation as the designer of a number of cover spreads for the press in Hong Kong and abroad and as an illustrator and creative designer of various Comic Books / Story Books .

He then stepped away from commercial work and devoted himself solely to Oil painting. In recent years, he has aesthetically moved away from a stylistic "Icons Photorealist" to HongKonger-Realism, pushing his rendered subjects into a mythological arena. His artistic visions are treasured and collected by many . From there, Law quickly gained recognition in the art world by exhibiting at Hong Kong Convention and Exhibition Centre , The Avenue of Stars ; Law´s works are also appreciated and collected by many Hong Kong and international collectors.

Some of Law's Religious artworks for Catholic Church of Hong Kong are also gained media attention in 2006 and 2007 ,and was also received by the Cardinal of the Catholic Church in the same year .

His Pale Hair Girls are a thoroughly subversive tribute to the world of appearances worshipers and to the Hong Kong's Millennial Generation culture of 21 century, with which the painter has cultivated an almost ritualistic relationship. His paintings provoke and compel. There is a unique realness in spirit.

The artist lives and works at Central District , Hong Kong.

Solo Show at NatureArt Gallery

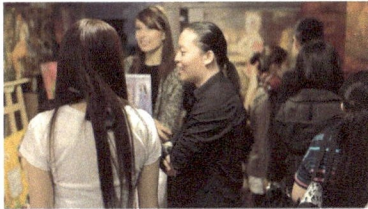

At Ceremony with the Cardinal

Painting by Michael Andrew Law

Michael Andrew Law

(852) 6444-7550
info@michaelandrewlaw.com
www.michaelandrewlaw.com

HONORS AND AWARDS:
*Medici Cast Study Recognized by Social Fine Arts Grade Examination Center Of China Academy Of Art.
*Social Fine Arts Grade Examination Center Of China Academy Of Art Promotional Art(2011-present)
Publishers Weekly Best illustrated 's Coffe Book 2004 (Pete M.Parks)
The Salt and The Light Catholic Church Children Book 2004 (Mars)
Borders Magazine Most Original Voices nominee 2006 (Dear Fish)
Publisher's Weekly Best Children's Book list 2004 (America the Beautiful)
Communication Digital Artist -- Award of Excellence
European Print Weekly Design Annual Awards (2000,2002)
Face to face Dolphin art competition silver award 2006
Art Directors of HKC Award of Merit (2005)
Society of Fine Art -- An exhibitor 2005 Society of Newspaper Design Award of Excellence
Michael and Stephanie Duo Exhibition (2006)
Spectrum Fantastic Art Annual (multiple)
not-for-profit aution for Rotary of HK 2012

Art Funtion for
Organic Beauty opening

Exhibition :
2013 DeTour Matters 2013 Satellite Events at NatureArt Gallery
2013 December to Remember , One man show at NatureArt Gallery Central District, Hong Kong.
2012 Solo Show , Park Central tseung kwan O ,Hong Kong
2011 Art Walk Group Showing , Discovery Bay ,Hong Kong
2011 HK Gold Coast (Book signing exhibition)
2009 Solo Painting Exhibition The Avenue of Stars
Group Exhibition of Daniel Anderson workshop Classical Realism class of 2008 at Manhattan,NY
2007 Guest and ExhibitionThe Peak Galleria Hong Kong
2007 Invited workshop exhibition, Elements, Hong Kong
Group Exhibition of Classical Realism class of 2007 at Manhattan,NY
2006 Collection by Cardinal Zen Ze-kiun and exhibited at Catholic Church of Hong Kong.
2004 - 2007, Hong Kong Young Artist Group Exhibition, Hong Kong Central Library.
Group Exhibition of Classical Realism class of 2006 at East Village, Manhattan,NY
2005 Illustration original exhibition for Kung Kao Po
2004 Group Exhibition, Wanchai Tower
2003 Group Exhibition, Hong Kong Convention and Exhibition Centre.
2003 Winner of I luv Hong Kong Painting Competition, exhibition at The Landmark (Hong Kong).
2002 The Holy story Picture Book illustrated picture original exhibition ,sai wan ho civic centre.

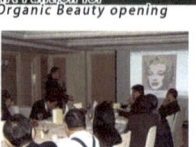

Art Funtion at
The Peninsula Hong Kong

SELECTED COLLECTIONS :
Cardinal of the Catholic Church Joseph Zen Ze-kiun
Organic Beauty Inc
Agriculture, Fisheries and Conservation Department
Ms.Ho Wei Ying
Ms. Annie Yu
Daniel Anderson
MR.Tsang Yan Sam

Interview with Hollywood Film
Producer / Teacher Dov Simens

PUBLICATIONS :
Fisheye magazine , featured artist interview , November 2002 (ISBN: N/A)
Kung Kao Po , interview , June 2006 (ISBN: N/A)
Art of Rock Realism , 2008 (ISBN: N/A)
Michael Andrew Law Early works Volume 1 - 3 :
(ISBN-13: 978-1503319400)
(ISBN-13: 978-1503366060)
(ISBN-13: 978-1503365087)
The Pale Hair Girls of Michael Andrew Law , 2010 (ISBN-13: 9781503372115)
December to Remember One man Show Art Book , 2013 (ISBN-13: 9781505609257)
Christmas Everyday : Pale Hair Girls Christmas Series 1 (ISBN-13: 978-1505453218)
Christmas Everyday : Pale Hair Girls Christmas Series 2 (ISBN-13: 978-1505467796)
Christmas Everyday : Pale Hair Girls Christmas Series 3 (ISBN-13: 978-1505468052)
Christmas Everyday : Pale Hair Girls Christmas Series 4 (ISBN-13: 978-1505470741)
Christmas Everyday : Pale Hair Girls Christmas Series 5 (ISBN-13: 978-1505470857)
Christmas Everyday : Pale Hair Girls Christmas Series 6 (ISBN-13: 978-1505471151)
Christmas Everyday : Pale Hair Girls Christmas Series Specials (ISBN-13: 978-1505583922)
I-Egoism by Michael Andrew Law (ISBN:978-1-4990-2124-0)

Exhibition at
Hong Kong Central Library.

Group Exhibition at
Hong Kong Museum of Art

Exhibition at Avenue of Stars; Hong Kong (2010)

Exhibition at Hong Kong
Convention and Exhibition Centre.

關於藝術家MICHAEL ANDREW LAW:

生長於交接時期香港的年輕藝術家 Michael Andrew Law，擅長把數碼繪圖，Pop 摩登藝術及古典油畫揉合時事及諷刺，創出獨特的視覺藝術語言及內容，跨越中西混合背景思維界限，探索互聯網世代交錯回歸的中西混雜之香港歷史。

他以自由隨意的手法結合摩登及古典材料與技巧，保持表現與認知、控制與隨性、魯妄與機智、自我與社羣等對立美學力量之間的張力，並對香港Y世代、本土文化及民族社會的殘酷現實作出尖刻的評論。Michael Andrew Law 的作品色彩豐富，寫實風格描繪的冰山美人，刻畫在滿佈流行文化圖像、東方書法標誌及符號的背景上。《白髮女孩系列》(The Pale Hair Girls，2006 — 2013 年) 的創作之中，Michael Andrew Law 獨特的繪畫風格呈獻出達達主義思考方式般的且出人意表的效果。畫中冰山美人式的人物穿插在抽象的香港和俗世符號上。

Pale Hair Girls系列的畫作的視覺靈感大量源自法國美術學院派大師William-Adolphe Bouguereau 的少年油畫作品以及已故華裔畫家陳逸飛的史詩及美人作品，Michael Andrew Law一反傳統的繪畫技法，以數碼混合古典繪畫技，重新演繹細緻複雜的中西方古典畫面和精心細緻思考的構圖，以西式媒介呼應中國的傳統書法裡作為圖案之筆觸，在 Michael Andrew Law的筆下這種交錯西式POP ART和中式古典藝術表現時輪廓卻非常細緻，尤其最廣為流傳和臨摹的Leonardo da Vinci作品Mona Lisa (1517 年)，以東方血統之妻子肖像取代Mona Lisa 的表徵意義，極具質感的厚顏料同時呈現寫生畫作時人物肉體的細微變化。

《誰會理會不是自已的新天地:三聯畫》（Humanity）刻畫了在世代末日的未來世代們於本為廢墟的香港島上，等待著他們的命運。這些離奇的場景與Jerry B. Jenkins及Timothy LaHaye等當代作家描寫的超現實、宗教解讀、未來主義情懷如出一致。於半島酒店扶輪會演講當代藝術

主要探索他藝術裡其中一項最重要的二分法：浪漫與嘲諷、作為藝術家對美的浪漫思考與交滙中西混合背景思維之香港Y世代的悲情，由天真燦爛的冰山美人式少女與可怕的末日和俗物之間的強烈對比作像徵。無論是標誌性的單幅「古典書法圖案的無身份肖像」，抑或以三聯畫形式出現，運用到大師級繪畫與構圖技巧，揉合了精細傳統油畫技法與摩登畫的表現方式建構，美人亦在美術史和流行文化裡是永恆的主題。冰山美人式少女令人聯想到生命的脆弱與時光飛逝之無情。藝術家就是要了解不同世界之間的界線並翻譯到不同文化價值之間的語境如高尚對低俗、古代對現代、東方對西方。

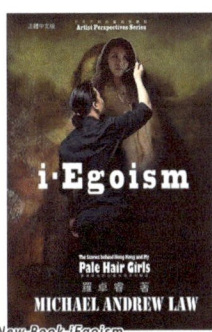

New Book iEgoism
ISBN:978-1-4990-2124-0

憑著 iEgoism 故事性的風格和精神，Michael Andrew Law將流行、古典與時事內容混合成一種感覺超豐富的視覺藝術作品，所涉獵的美學領域和文化靈感不斷延伸，而他在當中游走自如。一如常見的當代藝術主題，去作為「諷刺」及「反思」有關「浪漫」與「悲情」的直接敘述。

他所開發的iEgoism主題，就深受當代或反傳統藝術愛好者的喜愛，這被視為跟西方DADA藝術主義互相呼應。Michael Andrew Law把自己置身於他熱烈的自我網世代主義- iEgoism裡展現出的姿態卻是完全屬於他本人和他的時代的。

Michael Andrew Law於2006 年隨美國紐約藝術家Daniel Anderson深造古典油畫，其後發展純美術繪畫工作，2008年獲贊助於香港中環成立藝術工作室 Nature Art。除了製作藝術及相關作品，Nature Art 及 Michael Andrew Law 亦積極培育香港年輕藝術家。

2013 年，他於NatureArt Gallery舉行藝術展覽《iEgoism》，從香港歷史中追溯當代香港流行視覺藝術文化的特徵。

Michael Andrew Law 的作品曾於紐約 Chelsea 的聯合展覽中展出，他亦曾在著名機構及學校舉行個展及講座，例如星光大道 (2009 年)、天主教香港教區、香港中央圖書館(2004 -2007 年)、灣仔政府大樓外(2004 年)，香港會議展覽中心 (2003 年)。2015出版藝術文字著作《不可不知的藝術家觀點系列-iEgoism》更深入探討香港Y世代、香港歷史和Michael Andrew Law的作品脈絡關聯。

Michael Andrew Law 現於香港定居及從事創作。

Michael Andrew Law fusing digital and classical painting with west and East creative philosophy , to produce an extremely original artistic language and content that bridged west and east ,classical and modern medium , at the same time clearly tells the stories of his own generation. Combining digital creative materials and classical painting techniques with effusive yet knowing and precise focused , his paintings maintain a powerful tension between opposing aesthetic forces—expression and knowledge, control and spontaneity, savagery and wit, urbanity and primitivism—while providing satiric commentary on the oppressive realities of the predicament of Generation Internet, homegrown hongkonger's local-culture vesus Traditional Chinese culture, and The Hong Kong's post-handover history.

In his dynamically designed compositions, gracefully detailed figures and innocent faces are incise against fields that juxtaposed with portraits, chinese calligraphy, and sometimes cgi. The Pale Hair Girls Series (2006 - 2013) depicts realistic cold, icy-like young female figures surrounded by abstract and expressively painted forms and shapes revealing images of Pop culture, Historial figures, and Hong Kong landmarks.

Michael Andrew Law draws inspiration from Old Master's works such as Caravaggio , Ruben , Rembrandt , all the way to the Modern Art Superstars such as Warhol , Lichtenstein , Richter , De Kooning , Bacon , Wool and Prince . The Pale Hair Girls series mainly inspired by the painting works of French academic painter and traditionalist William-Adolphe Bouguereau and the Late Great YiFei Chen's characteristic "Romantic Realism" paintings.

In a reversal of standard East-West aesthetics, Law re-interprets Old Master's sophisticated imagery combine classical and digital materials—which resonate with Digital Vector Designs and Paintings—with fine strokes of oil paint multi-layered with paint film.In his interpretation of Leonardo Da Vinci's iconic Mona Lisa's smile (1517)—an iconic image that has been endlessly disseminated and reproduced—Law painted over the symbolism of the portrait Mona Lisa with his young wife , intent on rendering the figure in contemporary fashion with the iconic image as background .

 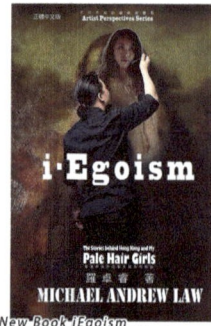

New Book iEgoism
ISBN:978-1-4990-2124-0

"The Humanity triptych" depicts New Generation HongKongers in a Ruined Hong Kong city , awaiting their unknown fate of a new beginning. This painting series explores one of the central paradox of his art—between romance and derision , his romantic magnanimity as an artist and his pessimistic perspective on the predicament of Generation Y Hongkongers. Here, this paradox is symbolized by the stark contrast of icy cold young female and disturbing representations of the armageddon-like of images. Whether portrayed as single "chinese calligraphy " or in triptych composition and classical paintwork that combine both expressive and traditional painting techniques with the digital vector , the beauties and the human figures stand as eternal motifs in the history of art and also in popular culture. Both oppositional and parallel, they are reminders of the fragile vibrancy of life and the impitoyable passing of time.

A references between different cultural refrence (high/pop, classical/contemporary, east/west), Michael Andrew Law has stated that an artist should be someone who understood how to hybrid between different worlds and go ahead makes an effort to knowing them. With his distinctive "iEgoism" philosophy , which employs highly refined academic painting techniques to depict a mixture of abstract expressionism within a representational pop culture images. These techniques parallel to the themes of romance and predicament of this generation , he recollects and revitalizes narratives of irony and introspection.

Michael Andrew Lawwas born in 1982 in British Hong Kong , studied fine art with american artist Daniel Anderson and graduate of China Central Academy of Fine Arts Sam Zeng from 2003 - 2006 . He co-founded the Hong Kong Art Studio Nature Art Workshop in 2008. In addition to the production and marketing of Michael Andrew Law's art and related work, Nature Art functions as a supportive environment for the fostering of emerging Hong Konger artists. Law is also a curator. In 2013, he organized an exhibition of contemporary art titled "iEgoism ," which served as a narration of contemporary HongKong Gen Y pop culture .

從荷理活看藝術圈哲學

在荷理活今天，大約有十萬個演員，其中大約有二萬個是正職報稱是演戲的，名字能賣[不管能賣多少]的該不到一千人，一般人能記得的不到五百人吧，一年內在大電影海報掛名主演的不到二佰位，能真正賺大錢的富豪級不到一佰位，這是事實。

當然，其他二萬個是正職報稱是演戲的無名之士中，收入相當可觀亦大有人在，即是不是富豪級亦比下有餘，那其他十萬人呢？ 他們是演員，有時是貨車司機，有時是侍應，有時是文員，有時是無業遊民，是在等待機會的一群。

要從十萬人一群流動到那二萬正職的一群，首先是要忍耐亦是要專注，關鍵詞就是「想辦法，捱過去」，其他則一點科學也沒有，不論你是學院畢業，碩士，自學，甚至連一點理論技巧也沒有，一點關系也沒有，唯一就是想辦法捱過去，直至演戲可以成為主要收入。

好了，恭喜成為二萬位正職是演戲的人，又怎麼了，不代表你演技很好，不代表你再幹下去十年後就可升到Johnny DEPP的位置，成為二萬位正職是演戲的人只代表你以表演的收入作為生活開支的主源已。

那麼，如何才能成為名字能賣的一仟幾百人之一呢？ 這個則開始到了連公式也靠不住了級數，

當然，若你真正想做的就只是演戲，能當荷理活二萬位正職是演戲的人之一已對得起列祖列宗吧，但若你只是想當明星，也

是有方法，能跳過「捱過」十萬個演員之列直接成為大電影海報掛名主演的不到二佰位之一的，方法之一:去贏個運動金牌，Arnold Schwarzenegger，The Rock 就是這樣上位，方法之二:嫁個名人，Ann Nicole Smith 就是這樣當上主角，方法之三:故意製新聞話題者則例如Paris Hilton，或香港的周秀娜，方法之四:故意靠近高層人脈，著他們讓你上位，亦有其他千奇百怪之上位方案而不便在此詳列，當然，這些方法，即使讓你成功上位了也不是100%可靠，因為如此行捷徑進入演戲界後再獲成功者亦屬罕有，除了因為外人空降到圈內會立刻成為眾矢之的，也要在表演上在售票立場上站得住腳；也可以有些人是一輩子做儘各方法之後也不能成為那一仟幾百人之一的也有；結論就是，在苦幹之後，就唯有靠上帝了:這就是藝圈。

反過來從荷理活演員那個環境，回看到香港，幹藝術該用甚麼哲學呢？

Michael Andrew Law
(852) 6444-7550
info@michaelandrewlaw.com
www.michaelandrewlaw.com

Selected publications

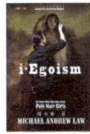

iEgoism by Michael Andrew Law
Softcover : 110 pages
Publisher : Xlibris LLC
ISBN: Softcover 978-1-4990-2124-0
ISBN: EBook 978-1-4990-2118-9

Michael Andrew Law The early years volume one: Nine Drawings from the early years collection
ISBN-10: 1503319407
ISBN-13: 978-1503319400

Michael Andrew Law The early years volume Two: Nine more Drawings from the early years collection (Volume 2)
ISBN-10: 1503365085
ISBN-13: 978-1503365087

Michael Andrew Law The early years volume Three: Nine Drawings from the early years collection (Volume 3)
ISBN-10: 1503366065
ISBN-13: 978-1503366060
Product Dimensions: 6 x 0.1 x 9 inches

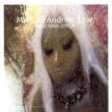

Michael Andrew Law: Pale Hair Girls Catalogue (Volume 1)
Paperback: 124 pages
ISBN-10: 1503372111
ISBN-13: 978-1503372115
Product Dimensions: 8.5 x 0.3 x 8.5 inches

December To Remember: Michael Andrew Law Exhibition
Paperback: 120 pages
ISBN-10: 1505609259
ISBN-13: 978-1505609257

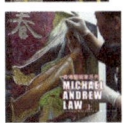

Hong Kong Artist Series: Michael Andrew Law 1
Paperback: 48 pages
ISBN-10: 1507580665
ISBN-13: 978-1507580660

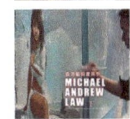

Hong Kong Artist Series: Michael Andrew Law 2'
Paperback: 48 pages
ISBN-10: 1507581556
ISBN-13: 978-1507581551

Michael Andrew Law

(852) 6444-7550
info@michaelandrewlaw.com
www.michaelandrewlaw.com

Publications : Illustrated Books

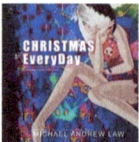

Christmas Everyday Book 1: Pale Hair Girls Christmas Series (Pale Hair Girls Christmas Everyday) (Volume 1)

ISBN-10: 1505453216

ISBN-13: 978-1505453218

Product Dimensions: 8.5 x 0.1 x 8.5 inches

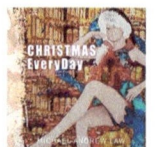

Christmas Everyday Book 2: Pale Hair Girls Christmas Series (Pale Hair Girls Christmas Everyday) (Volume 2)

ISBN-10: 1505467799

ISBN-13: 978-1505467796

Product Dimensions: 8.5 x 0.1 x 8.5 inches

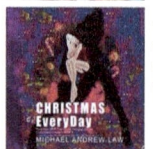

Christmas Everyday Book 3: Pale Hair Girls Christmas Series (Pale Hair Girls Christmas Everyday) (Volume 3)

ISBN-10: 1505468051

ISBN-13: 978-1505468052

Product Dimensions: 8.5 x 0.1 x 8.5 inches

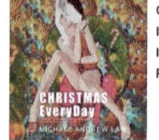

Christmas Everyday Book 4: Pale Hair Girls Christmas Series (Pale Hair Girls Christmas Everyday) (Volume 4)

ISBN-10: 1505470749

ISBN-13: 978-1505470741

Product Dimensions: 8.5 x 0.1 x 8.5 inches

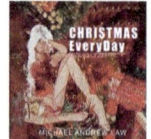

Christmas Everyday Book 5: Pale Hair Girls Christmas Series (Pale Hair Girls Christmas Everyday) (Volume 5)

ISBN-10: 1505470854

ISBN-13: 978-1505470857

Product Dimensions: 8.5 x 0.1 x 8.5 inches

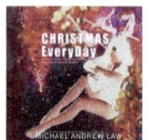

Christmas Everyday Book 6: Pale Hair Girls Christmas Series (Pale Hair Girls Christmas Everyday) (Volume 6)

ISBN-10: 150547115X

ISBN-13: 978-1505471151

Product Dimensions: 8.5 x 0.1 x 8.5 inches

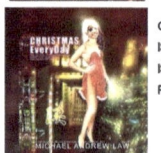

Christmas Everyday: Special Edition (Pale Hair Girls Christmas Everyday) (Volume 7)

ISBN-10: 1505583926

ISBN-13: 978-1505583922

Product Dimensions: 8.5 x 0.3 x 8.5 inches

Michael Andrew Law

(852) 6444-7550
info@michaelandrewlaw.com
www.michaelandrewlaw.com

Selected Works for Art Events

iEgoism Exhibition at NatureArt ,Central District Hong Kong

iEgoism Exhibition In Photos (from left) : TV/ Movie stars Cherrie Kong ,Michael Andrew Law , Iva law ,Florence Lawman.

Michael Andrew Law exhibition at the Avenue of Stars, Hong Kong (星光大道).

Michael Andrew Law exhibition at the Avenue of Stars, Hong Kong (星光大道).

Art Related Events for Organic Beauty opening,

Art Talks at Credit Agricole CIB, Hong Kong Branch

Art Talks for The Rotary Club of Hong Kong At The Peninsula Hong Kong

Michael Andrew Law

(852) 6444-7550
info@michaelandrewlaw.com
www.michaelandrewlaw.com

Selected Works for Art Events

As Guest Art Tutor at Diocesan Boys' School

Working With Film Producer & Founder of Hollywood Film Institute Dov Simens.

Art Competition Award ceremony with Dr. Sarah Mary Liao , then-Secretary for the Environment of the Hong Kong Special Administrative Region .

Self Curated Exhibition with Art Collectors at Art Center ,2005.

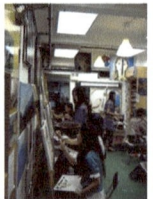
Curated Art Events with The Swire Group (太古集團).

Curated Art Events with Hong Kong Stock Exchange (香港交易所).

Michael Andrew Law

(852) 6444-7550
info@michaelandrewlaw.com
www.michaelandrewlaw.com

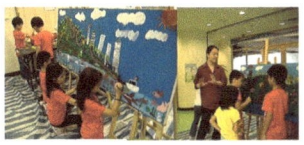

Art Event with Young Men's Christian Association (YMCA).

Group Exhibition, Hong Kong Convention and Exhibition Centre.

iEgoism Exhibition

Exhibition, Elements, Hong Kong

Oil Painting Shown in magazine :
壹周刊第1047期]第 20屆壹電視大獎 – 謝雪心

Michael Andrew Law

(852) 6444-7550
info@michaelandrewlaw.com
www.michaelandrewlaw.com

Selected Works for Art Events

Art Talk and Exhibition at Pui Shing Catholic Secondary School.

Art Talks and Charity Auction for The Rotary Club of Hong Kong At The Peninsula Hong Kong

Cardinal Zen Ze-kiun receives Michael Andrew Law at Ceremony. Comission portrait by Catholic Church of Hong Kong

Michael Andrew Law

(852) 6444-7550
info@michaelandrewlaw.com
www.michaelandrewlaw.com

The Pale Hair Universe Series

Medium : Traditional Oil Painting (With Acrylic Based) , Glitter , Gold Leaf .
About This Serie : Created Along with the First Series of painting of The
Pale Hair Girls Original Series Paintings , Done with mixed media on canvas ,
with classical painting method.
Number of Paintings : 7 (As of 2015)
Availability : Limited Edition , Prints , Original Painting

Michael Andrew Law

(852) 6444-7550
info@michaelandrewlaw.com
www.michaelandrewlaw.com

Pale Hair Girls Original Series.

Medium : Traditional Oil Painting (With Acrylic Based) , Glitter , Gold Leaf .
About This Serie : First Series of painting of The entire Pale Hair Girls Universe ,
done with mixed media on canvas , with classical painting method.
Number of Paintings : 60 (As of 2015)
Availability : Limited Edition , Prints , Original Painting

Details

info@michaelandrewlaw.com
www.michaelandrewlaw.com

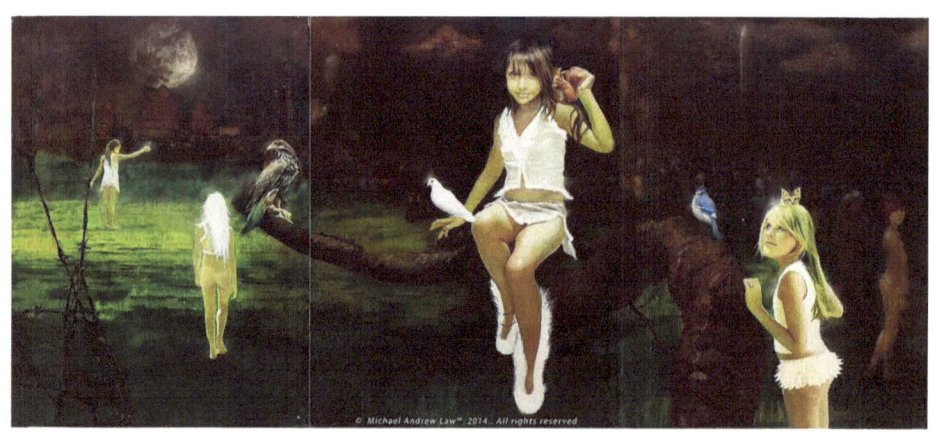

4'x 9' Multi-Panel Painting

info@michaelandrewlaw.com
www.michaelandrewlaw.com
© Michael Andrew Law™ 2014.All rights reserved

30x20 ″ oil on canvas

S-P-R-I-N-G

info@michaelandrewlaw.com
www.michaelandrewlaw.com

© Michael Andrew Law™ 2014.All rights reserved

48x36 ˝ oil on canvas

Nothing stops dreams

info@michaelandrewlaw.com
www.michaelandrewlaw.com

© Michael Andrew Law™ 2014.All rights reserved

4'x 9' Multi-Panel Painting

info@michaelandrewlaw.com
www.michaelandrewlaw.com

© Michael Andrew Law™ 2014.All rights reserved

32x46 ″ oil on canvas

Somewhere beyond my reach

info@michaelandrewlaw.com
www.michaelandrewlaw.com

36x48 ″ oil on canvas

Goodbye Future II

info@michaelandrewlaw.com
www.michaelandrewlaw.com

30x30 ˝ oil on canvas

I only dreams cause I am Alive.

info@michaelandrewlaw.com
www.michaelandrewlaw.com

Michael Andrew Law

(852) 6444-7550
info@michaelandrewlaw.com
www.michaelandrewlaw.com

Pale Hair Girls : The New

Medium : Mixed Media Painting (oil and Acrylic) , Glitter , Gold Leaf .
About This Serie : Second Series of painting of The entire Pale Hair Girls Universe ,
done with mixed media on canvas , classical method crossover with contemporary Digital painting method.
Number of Paintings : 80 (As of 2015)
Availability : Limited Edition , Prints , Special Edition .

Michael Andrew Law

(852) 6444-7550
info@michaelandrewlaw.com
www.michaelandrewlaw.com

Pale Hair Girls : The New

Medium : Mixed Media Painting (oil and Acrylic) , Glitter , Gold Leaf .
About This Serie : Second Series of painting of The entire Pale Hair Girls Universe ,
done with mixed media on canvas , classical method crossover with contemporary Digital
painting method.
Number of Paintings : 80 (As of 2015)
Availability : Limited Edition , Prints , Special Edition .

Michael Andrew Law

(852) 6444-7550
info@michaelandrewlaw.com
www.michaelandrewlaw.com

Pale Hair Girls : Christmas Everyday

Medium : Mixed Media Painting (digital print with Acrylic) , Glitter , Gold Leaf .
About This Serie : Special Series illustrations of The Pale Hair Girls Universe ,
done with mixed media on canvas , classical method crossover with contemporary Digital
painting method.
Number of Paintings : 102 (As of 2015)
Availability : Limited Edition , Prints , Special Edition .

Forgive the guilty.

am I allowed to go Christmas shopping?

Peace on earth will come to stay, when we live Christmas every day

How all of our hopes Had come down to this child

Michael Andrew Law

(852) 6444-7550
info@michaelandrewlaw.com
www.michaelandrewlaw.com

Pale Hair Girls : iEgoism

Medium : Mixed Media Painting (oil and Acrylic) , Glitter , Gold Leaf .
About This Serie : Third Series of painting of The entire Pale Hair Girls Universe ,
done with mixed media on canvas , classical method crossover with contemporary painting method.
Number of Paintings : 960 (As of 2015)
Availability : Limited Edition , Prints , Special Edition .

Michael Andrew Law

(852) 6444-7550
info@michaelandrewlaw.com
www.michaelandrewlaw.com

Pale Hair Girls : iEgoism

Medium : Mixed Media Painting (oil and Acrylic) , Glitter , Gold Leaf .
About This Serie : Third Series of painting of The entire Pale Hair Girls Universe ,
done with mixed media on canvas , classical method crossover with contemporary painting method.
Number of Paintings : 960 (As of 2015)
Availability : Limited Edition , Prints , Special Edition .

MIC...ND...

Limited Edition
限量版畫現已接受訂購
Available on Demand

We ❤ MICHAEL ANDREW LAW

A Hong Kong contemporary artists

Michael Andrew Law at Work.

Michael Andrew Law fusing digital and classical painting with west and East creative philosophy , to produce an extremely original artistic language and content that bridged west and east ,classical and modern medium , at the same time clearly tells the stories of his own generation. Combining digital creative materials and classical painting techniques with effusive yet knowing and precise focused , his paintings maintain a powerful tension between opposing aesthetic forces—expression and knowledge, control and spontaneity, savagery and wit, urbanity and primitivism—while providing satiric commentary on the oppressive realities of the predicament of Generation Internet, homegrown hongkonger's local-culture vesus Traditional Chinese culture, and The Hong Kong's post-handover history.

In his dynamically designed compositions, gracefully detailed figures and innocent faces are incise against fields that juxtaposed with portraits, chinese calligraphy, and sometimes cgi. The Pale Hair Girls Series (2006 - 2013) depicts realistic cold, icy-like young female figures surrounded by abstract and expressively painted forms and shapes revealing images of Pop culture, Historial figures, and Hong Kong landmarks.

Michael Andrew Law draws inspiration from Old Master's works such as Caravaggio , Ruben , Rembrandt , all the way to the Modern Art Superstars such as Warhol , Lichtenstein , Richter , De Kooning , Bacon , Wool and Prince . The Pale Hair Girls series mainly inspired by the painting works of French academic painter and traditionalist William-Adolphe Bouguereau and the Late Great YiFei Chen's characteristic "Romantic Realism" paintings.

In a reversal of standard East-West aesthetics, Law re-interprets Old Master's sophisticated imagery combine classical and digital materials—which resonate with Digital Vector Designs and Paintings—with fine strokes of oil paint multi-layered with paint film.In his interpretation of Leonardo Da Vinci's iconic Mona Lisa's smile (1517)—an iconic image that has been endlessly disseminated and reproduced—Law painted over the symbolism of the portrait Mona Lisa with his young wife , intent on rendering the figure in contemporary fashion with the iconic image as background .

"The Humanity triptych" depicts New Generation HongKongers in a Ruined Hong Kong city , awaiting their unknown fate of a new beginning. This painting series explores one of the central paradox of his art—between romance and derision , his romantic magnanimity as an artist and his pessimistic perspective on the predicament of Generation Y Hongkongers. Here, this paradox is symbolized by the stark contrast of icy cold young female and disturbing representations of the armageddon-like of images. Whether portrayed as single "chinese calligraphy " or in triptych composition and classical paintwork that combine both expressive and traditional painting techniques with the digital vector , the beauties and the human figures stand as eternal motifs in the history of art and also in popular culture. Both oppositional and parallel, they are reminders of the fragile vibrancy of life and the impitoyable passing of time.

A references between different cultural refrence (high/pop, classical/contemporary, east/west), Michael Andrew Law has stated that an artist should be someone who understood how to hybrid between different worlds and go ahead makes an effort to knowing them. With his distinctive "iEgoism" philosophy , which employs highly refined academic painting techniques to depict a mixture of abstract expressionism within a representational pop culture images. These techniques parallel to the themes of romance and predicament of this generation , he recollects and revitalizes narratives of irony and introspection.

Michael Andrew Law was born in 1982 in British Hong Kong , studied fine art with american artist Daniel Anderson and with artist graduatee of China Central Academy of Fine Arts Sam Zeng from 2003 - 2006 . He co-founded the Hong Kong Art Studio Nature Art Workshop in 2008. In addition to the production and marketing of Michael Andrew Law's art and related work, Nature Art functions as a supportive environment for the
fostering of emerging Hong Konger artists. Law is also a curator. In 2013, he organized an exhibition of contemporary art titled "iEgoism," which served as a commentaries of contemporary HongKong Gen Y pop culture ;These Theroy also published in the book : "iEgoism" in 2014.

Michael Andrew Law currently works and lives in Hong Kong.

For further information please contact the studio at info@michaelandrewlaw.com or at +852.6444.7550. All images are subject to copyright. Artist/Studio/Gallery's approval must be granted prior to reproduction.

2010 Avenue of Stars, Hong Kong

Exhibition :

2013 DeTour Matters 2013 Satellite Events at NatureArt Gallery
2013 December to Remember , One man show at NatureArt Gallery Central District, Hong Kong.
2012 Solo Show , Park Central tseung kwan O ,Hong Kong
2011 Art Walk Group Showing , Discovery Bay ,Hong Kong
2011 HK Gold Coast (Book signing exhibition)
2009 Solo Painting Exhibition The Avenue of Stars
Group Exhibition of Daniel Anderson workshop Classical Realism class of 2008 at Manhattan,NY
2007 Guest and Exhibition The Peak Galleria Hong Kong
2007 Invited workshop exhibition, Elements, Hong Kong
Group Exhibition of Classical Realism class of 2007 at Manhattan,NY
2006 Collection by Cardinal Zen Ze-kiun and exhibited at Catholic Church of Hong Kong.
2004 - 2007, Hong Kong Young Artist Group Exhibition, Hong Kong Central Library.
Group Exhibition of Classical Realism class of 2006 at East Village, Manhattan,NY
2005 Illustration original exhibition for Kung Kao Po
2004 Group Exhibition, Wanchai Tower
2003 Group Exhibition, Hong Kong Convention and Exhibition Centre,
2003 Winner of I luv Hong Kong Painting Competition, exhibition at The Landmark (Hong Kong).
2002 The Holy story Picture Book illustrated picture original exhibition ,sai wan ho civic centre.

SELECTED COLLECTIONS :

Cardinal of the Catholic Church Joseph Zen Ze-kiun
Organic Beauty Inc
Agriculture, Fisheries and Conservation Department
Ms.Ho Wei Ying
Ms. Annie Yu
Daniel Anderson
MR.Tsang Yan Sam

PUBLICATIONS :

Fisheye magazine , featured artist interview , November 2002
Kung Kao Po , interview , June 2006
Art of Rock Realism , 2008
The Art of Michael Andrew Law , 2010
December to Remember One man Show Art Book , 2013
iEgoism , 2015

Solo Shows 2010 - 2013

I really appreciate your purchase of this Painting

Collection Book , I hope you enjoy reading them as

much as I enjoyed painting them!

May God bless your home with peace, joy and love.

From Michael Andrew Law.

Find Me Online.

Michael Andrew Law 🔍

Available Now!

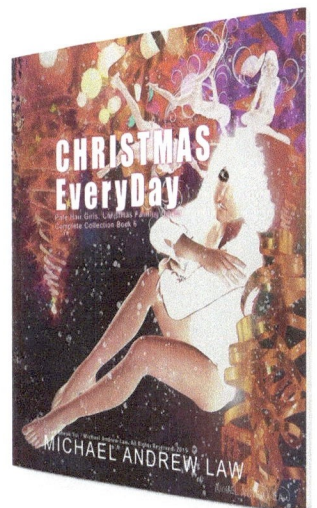

www.ingramcontent.com/pod-product-compliance
Lightning Source LLC
Chambersburg PA
CBHW040749200526
45159CB00025B/1823